IRON WILL

SURVIVING THE CAVE

Kristin J. Russo

full tilt PRESS

Surviving the Cave
ron Will

Copyright © 2020
Published by Full Tilt Press
Written by Kristin J. Russo
All rights reserved.

Printed in the United States of America.
No part of this book may be reproduced in any manner whatsoever without written permission, except in the case of brief quotations embodied in critical articles and reviews.

Full Tilt Press
42964 Osgood Road
Fremont, CA 94539
readfulltilt.com

Full Tilt Press publications may be purchased for educational, business, or sales promotional use.

Editorial Credits
Design and layout by Sara Radka
Edited by Lauren Dupuis-Perez
Copyedited by Renae Gilles

Image Credits
Getty Images: duckycards, 37 (energy bar), Design Pics RF, 37 (oxygen tank), EXTREME-PHOTOGRAPHER, 34, EyeEm, 33, iStockphoto, 15, 16, 17, 19, 22, 23, 35, Janine Lamontagne, 37 (water bottle), Johner RF, 3 (bats), 21, Kevin Winter, 13, 44 (bottom), Lawrence Manning, 36, Linh Pham, 3 (top), 9, 11, 44 (top), Matt Anderson Photography, background, Phuvich Chavitrutaigul, 43, ronniechua, 3 (bottom), 31, skodonnell, 45; NASA: GSFC/METI/ERSDAC/ AROS, and U.S./Japan ASTER Science Team, 28 (bottom); Newscom: MEGA/News Licensing, 7, NOTIMEX, 3 middle), 25, 27, 28 (top), 29; Pixabay: Free-Photos, 2 (background), picman2, cover (background), StockSnap, 4, TanteTati, 36 (rope), Wikimedialmages, 37 (flashlight); Shutterstock: Thomas Wong, cover (foreground)

SBN: 978-1-62920-807-7 (library binding)
SBN: 978-1-62920-815-2 (ePub)

CONTENTS

Surviving the Cave 4
Lost Together 6
Flash Flood Underground 12
Left Behind 18
Nine Days Underground 24
Double Trouble 30
The Stuff of Survival 36
Iron Will Stats 38
Map: Cave Systems 40
Iron Will 42
      Quiz 44
      Activity 45
      Glossary 46
      Read More 47
      Internet Sites 47
      Index 48

SURVIVING THE CAVE

Caves are large underground chambers. They are found all over the world. Some caves form when natural acid burns through rock. Others are formed by broken rock or boiling **magma**. **Stalactites** and **stalagmites** develop when minerals and water drip from cave ceilings. The minerals form spikes that hang from cave ceilings and rise from rocky floors. Waterfalls flow in enormous underground rooms. Caves are both dangerous and beautiful. **Spelunkers** climb through dark, narrow passages and slippery tunnels. They look for natural wonders that can only be found underground. But caving is risky. Even a small mistake can be deadly. One must have an **iron will** to survive the dangers below Earth's surface.

magma: hot liquid from below Earth's surface; lava and igneous rock are formed from magma

stalactite: a formation shaped like an icicle made from calcium salts that hangs from the ceiling of a cave

stalagmite: a mound or column made from calcium salts that rises from the floor of a cave

spelunker: a person who explores caves

iron will: having a strong feeling that you are going to do something and that you will not allow anything to stop you

SURVIVING THE CAVE 5

LOST TOGETHER

Thai soccer team
Tham Luang Caves
Thailand
2018

The Tham Luang caves are located under the Doi Nang Mountain range in the northernmost part of Thailand.

June 23, 2018, was Peerapat Sompiangjai's 16th birthday. He spent it doing what he loved most—playing soccer with his team, the Wild Boars. The team wanted to continue training when practice was over. Peerapat joined his coach, Ekkapol "Ake" Chantawong, and 11 teammates on a 45-minute bike ride to the Tham Luang caves.

The boys were going to hike through the dark tunnels. They only planned to go about 1.5 miles (2.4 kilometers) from the entrance. They didn't think it would take very long. "We only planned to spend one hour in the cave," said Coach Ake.

They left their bicycles at the entrance. When it was time to head home, the way out was flooded. Night was falling, and so were heavy rains. They were trapped.

> "We had faith that if we could not get out, someone would come in and get us."
>
> **EKKAPOL CHANTAWONG**

RISING WATER

The head coach discovered the team's bikes outside of the cave. He called for help. Rescuers raced to the site. Inside the cave, the boys hiked to higher ground. They had no food or water. Their belongings had been left with their bicycles. They found a rocky **ledge** that would keep them safe from the rising flood. The boys were hungry and tired. They could not drink the muddy water that pooled near their ledge. They licked **condensation** from the walls and the cave's stalactites.

Their only source of light was the flashlights they had brought with them. It wasn't long before the batteries died and the lights went out. The boys did not panic. Coach Ake had been a Buddhist **monk**. He showed the boys how to **meditate**. This helped calm their nerves. "We were not scared and we did not lose hope," said Ake. "We had faith that if we could not get out, someone would come in and get us."

ledge: a narrow, flat surface that juts out from a rock wall

condensation: water from the air that has settled onto a cool surface

monk: a religious person who separates from society to practice a spiritual way of living

meditate: to spend time thinking quietly in order to reflect on something or to relax

Rescuers worked around the clock to try and remove floodwaters from the cave system to save the trapped Thai soccer team.

HELP ARRIVES

Nine days after the boys disappeared, a team of British divers and Thai Navy SEALs found them as they meditated in the cold darkness.

"How many are you?" asked one of the rescuers.

Ardoon Sam-aon, 14, understood the question. He answered in English, "Thirteen!" The rescuers were thrilled. All of the boys and their coach were alive!

But how would they get out? The cave was still flooded. Rescuers came up with a complicated plan. Each boy was placed in a Sked—a waterproof, sleeping-bag-like container. Each boy wore a face mask that provided oxygen. The boys were **tethered** to their rescuer and **sedated** so that they would not panic while they were under the water. They were brought out of the cave one at a time. Each rescue took eight hours.

They were brought to a hospital in Chiang Rai. Some had to be treated for lung and ear infections. All of the boys and their coach survived.

BUDDHISM IN THAILAND

Buddhism is the official religion in Thailand. The religion was started in the 6th century BC by Prince Siddhartha of India, who meditated under a Bodhi tree. More than 95 percent of the people in Thailand practice Buddhism. There are about 300,000 Buddhist monks in Thailand. Most Buddhist men in Thailand under the age of 20 become a monk for a period of time.

---

tethered: tied to something

sedated: given medicine to decrease pain or to soothe anxiety

A former Navy SEAL diver, Saman Kunan, died during the difficult rescue. The Wild Boars soccer team honored his memory.

LOCATION
Tham Luang caves, Mae Sai, Chiang Rai Province, Thailand

SURVIVING THE CAVE **11**

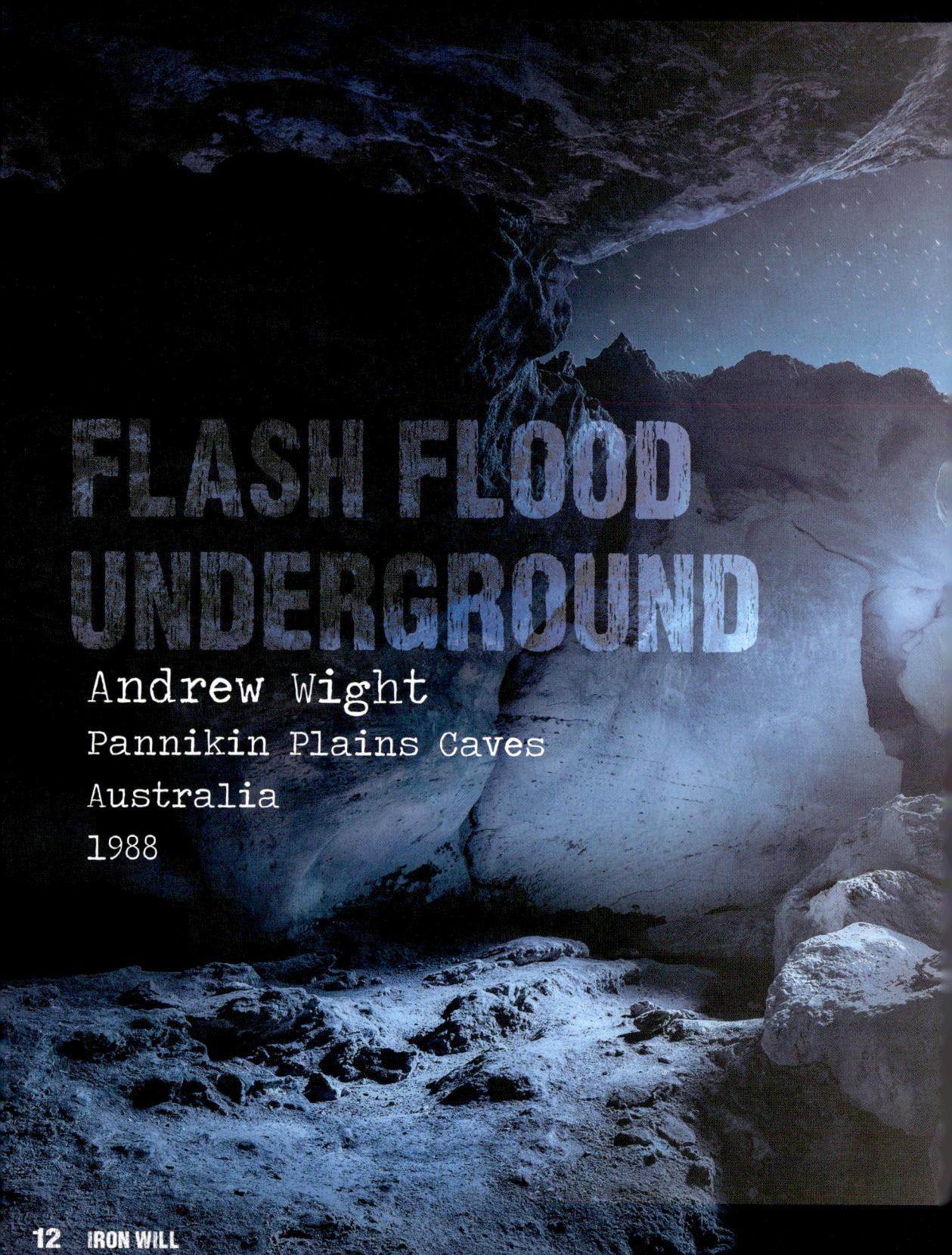

Andrew Wight started cave diving in Australia when he attended La Trobe University. He often filmed his adventures for television and documentaries.

In Western Australia, the Pannikin Plains cave system lies beneath the Nullarbor Plain. It is called the "Mount Everest" of caves. Andrew Wight and his team had travelled there to explore the caves. It was the last day of their trip. The group had pushed themselves to swim through deep, dark waters. They conquered dangerous tunnels and crawl spaces. Their hard work paid off. They saw natural wonders that few humans ever get to see. They were happy and satisfied with their accomplishments. It was time to go home.

"We were hauling the equipment out of the cave. We'd been out there for over a month," said Andrew. Without warning, disaster struck.

A surprise storm moved in and soaked the plains with heavy rain and hail the size of golf balls. The rainwater flooded the caves, trapping the cavers inside. For the next 27 hours, only their iron will would keep them alive.

"Do we stay on this little ledge and probably get sandwiched between the roof and the cave, which was collapsing? Or do we make a run for it and get killed that way?"

ANDREW WRIGHT

SURVIVING THE CAVE 13

TRAPPED

The **flash flood** made the cave collapse. The rocky ceiling fell. The walls and floor shifted. Andrew and his teammate Vicky Bonwick were separated from their group. **Rubble** and gushing water blocked their path.

"We were kind of in the middle section on a small ledge. We were trapped because there was no way down and no way out because of the water," said Andrew, "and the boulders were rolling around in the water. It was a question of do we stay on this little ledge and probably get sandwiched between the roof and the cave, which was collapsing? Or do we make a run for it and get killed that way?"

Andrew and Vicky didn't know if their friends were okay. Had they survived the cave's collapse? The pair followed a rope that had been put in place as a guideline. They dug their way through the rubble. They fought their way to the surface.

flash flood: a sudden, unexpected flood caused by heavy rain

rubble: broken fragments of rock

During a rockfall, thousands of pounds of rock can fall from the ceiling of a cave. Repeated rockfalls can cause entire caves to collapse.

THE STRUGGLE TO ESCAPE

Andrew and Vicky were able to escape from the cave. They called for help. Rescuers arrived and searched for the group trapped below. Andrew showed them where he thought they might be. "Everyone else was stuck much deeper in the cave in a larger chamber," said Andrew.

Rescuers found the trapped cavers. Now they had to find a way to get them out. "It was a process over the next two days of exploring a new way out of the cave," said Andrew. The cavers and their rescuers found a spot that they hoped would work. But they were afraid it might be dangerous. Moving rubble to make room for the rescue might cause more stones to fall. But they managed to clear a passageway. Rescuers lowered a guideline through the hole to the trapped cavers. The cavers scrambled up and out to safety. Finally, everyone was free.

DANGEROUS DESERT

Nullarbor Plain can be just as dangerous aboveground as it is belowground. It takes 6 days to drive 781 miles (1,257 km) through the desert-like plain. Although there are places along the road to buy supplies, visitors are encouraged to bring extra food, water, and fuel in case of an emergency. Nullarbor Plain is home to wild camels, kangaroos, and emus. From cliff tops, visitors can even see whales swimming in the ocean.

The Nullarbor Plain is located on the southwestern edge of Australia. Though it is near the ocean, the area is very dry and can be very dangerous for explorers.

SOUTH AUSTRALIA

LOCATION
Pannikin Plains caves, Nullarbor, South Australia, Australia

SURVIVING THE CAVE 17

LEFT BEHIND

Lukas Cavar
Sullivan Cave
Indiana, United States
2017

More than 43,000 students attend Indiana University.

"Help! Is anyone out there?"

LUKAS CAVAR

Lukas Cavar attended Indiana University in Bloomington, Indiana. He was a freshman there. He joined the Caving Club because he thought it would be a good way to meet new people. On Sunday, September 17, 2017, the club set out to Sullivan Cave.

Lukas was well prepared for his group's trip. It was only supposed to last half a day. He wore light clothes, knee and elbow pads, and hiking boots. In a plastic bag, he carried two bottles of water and two energy bars. He had an iPhone and headphones, his wallet, and a helmet with a headlight.

But three days later, Lukas was still in the cave. His food and water were long gone. His cell phone battery was dead. He was trapped and losing hope that he would ever be rescued.

ONE MISSED TURN

Each student was assigned a group and a buddy. Lukas and his buddy were in the second group. They explored the winding tunnels and tight passageways. But then, Lukas's group hit a low spot known as the "Backbreaker." Lukas decided to hurry through the challenge. He left his buddy and his group. He tried to catch up with the first group.

But he was not careful. He missed a turn that led to the exit. Eventually, he found the exit using arrows painted on the cave walls as his guide. But he made it to the gate too late. Everyone had left. Lukas was alone and locked inside.

"I was very confused and pretty scared," said Lukas. When darkness came, bats flew through the locked gate. Spiders and bats were all around him. He had no more water, so he licked condensation from the rocky walls. He thought about eating crickets. Night fell on his second day trapped in the cave. He curled into the **fetal position** to try to stay warm.

fetal position: the way a baby curls up in its mother's womb; a position that helps conserve body heat

A single colony of bats can include anywhere from a few dozen to a few thousand bats.

FRIENDS TO THE RESCUE

Lukas missed his classes on Monday. His friends became worried. Then he failed to show up for his job at the university's library on Tuesday. At that point, his friends knew something was terribly wrong. Lukas's parents filed a missing persons report when he failed to respond to their texts.

Campus police searched his room. They found muddy caving **gear** and assumed that Lukas had returned from the trip to Sullivan Cave. But they were wrong. When they realized that Lukas had been left behind, members of the Caving Club raced to the cave. They found Lukas. He was cold, tired, lonely, and afraid—but alive! They gave him a hamburger and a plate of pasta. "Probably the best food I've had in my life," Lukas said.

Caving gear can include a climbing harness, rope, and a helmet.

Lukas passed a medical exam at the cave. He said he did not want to go to the hospital. He wanted to go back to his dorm. His friends brought him back to campus. Lukas says he has no plans for any future spelunking trips.

---

gear: items such as tools, safety equipment, and other supplies needed to complete a task

MILES OF CAVES

There are caves in every state in the United States except Rhode Island and Louisiana. There about 17,000 caves in total. Cavers can explore about 125 of these caves. They are either run by the US National Park Service or they are privately owned. Mammoth Cave National Park in Kentucky is the longest cave system in world. There are flower-shaped minerals inside. It is also home to unusual animals such as blind fish and Kentucky cave shrimp.

LOCATION
Sullivan Cave, Springville, Indiana, United States

SURVIVING THE CAVE 23

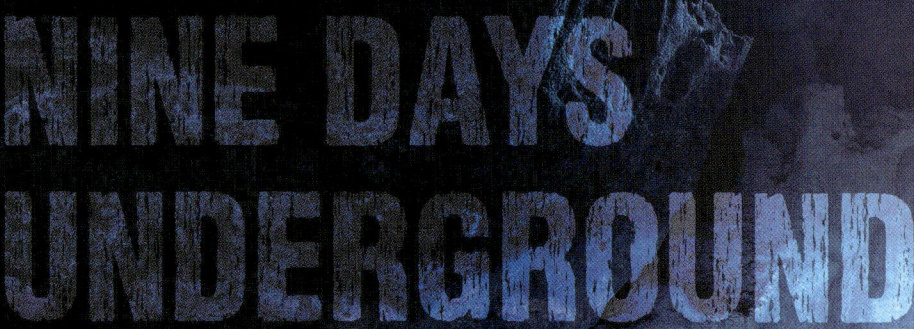

NINE DAYS UNDERGROUND

British Caving Association Members
Alpazat Caves
Puebla, Mexico
2004

Charles Milton was one of the group members to get trapped in the Cueva Alpazat caves.

"We kept talking about what we were going to eat after we got rescued, to keep up our morale, and we told each other our life stories."

JONATHAN SIMS

The Alpazat caves are located in Puebla, Mexico. Their underground passageways are a mystery. They include a 60-mile (97-km) network of caves. And they are mostly unmapped and unexplored. In 2004, a group of men travelled there together. The group included Jonathan Sims, John Roe, Charles Milton, Chris Mitchell, Toby Hamnett, and Simon Cornhill. They were members of the Combined Services Caving Association (CSCA) in Great Britain. They were all experienced cavers. They wanted to map some of the underground tunnels. The trip was planned for the dry season. There was less chance of rain during that time. But even experienced cavers can have bad luck. The men were deep inside the caves when a rainstorm struck. Flash floods aboveground meant disaster below. Rainwater flooded the **sumps** and blocked the exit. There was no way out.

sump: a pit where water collects

SURVIVING THE CAVE 25

BE PREPARED

The cavers were prepared for trouble. They had brought five days' worth of food with them. They knew that another group had visited the cave before them. That group had stashed another five days' worth of **rations** inside the cave. The CSCA cavers also brought sleeping bags, radios, and books to read.

When the flash flood trapped them inside, they called for help using a "mole" telephone. This is a special telephone. It can be used in areas with no cell service. After they called for help, they were still stuck. So the cavers passed the time playing cards. They made their own deck by ripping a piece of paper into 52 pieces.

"We were very hungry," said Jonathan Sims. "We kept talking about what we were going to eat after we got rescued, to keep up our morale, and we told each other our life stories."

A team of British divers helped plan the rescue. One of them, Rick Stanton, later helped to rescue the Thai soccer team trapped inside the Tham Luang caves in 2018. The team worked with Mexican rescuers to free the trapped cavers. Finally, after nine days underground, the group was free.

---

ration: a supply of food

British scientists John Taylor and Stevie Welsh were part of the rescue team trying to free the trapped Alpazat cavers.

SURVIVING THE CAVE 27

FAR FROM HOME

But there was another issue after they were rescued. Most of the CSCA cavers were members of the British military. Mexican officials became suspicious. The cavers had been mapping the caves. The Mexican officials thought this might be part of a military operation. **Foreign** militaries are not allowed to train in Mexico without permission. This meant that the cavers could not go home right away.

They had to wait in an **immigration** center in Mexico. British officials worked to help them gain permission to return home. They had already been trapped in the cave for nine days. They spent five more waiting at the immigration center. But finally, the cavers were allowed to fly home to Great Britain.

Homemade cards kept Jonathan Sims and the rest of the team entertained while they waited for rescue in the cave.

CAVE OF THE CRYSTALS

Mexico is home to one of the hottest caves on Earth. The Cave of the Crystals in Chihuahua averages 112° Fahrenheit (44° Celsius). A pool of magma beneath the cave makes it hot. The heat makes the cave difficult to explore.

foreign: from another country

immigration: the act of moving from one country to another

Two British rescuers helped the cavers escape the flooded passageways.

LOCATION
Alpazat Caves, Puebla, Mexico

SURVIVING THE CAVE 29

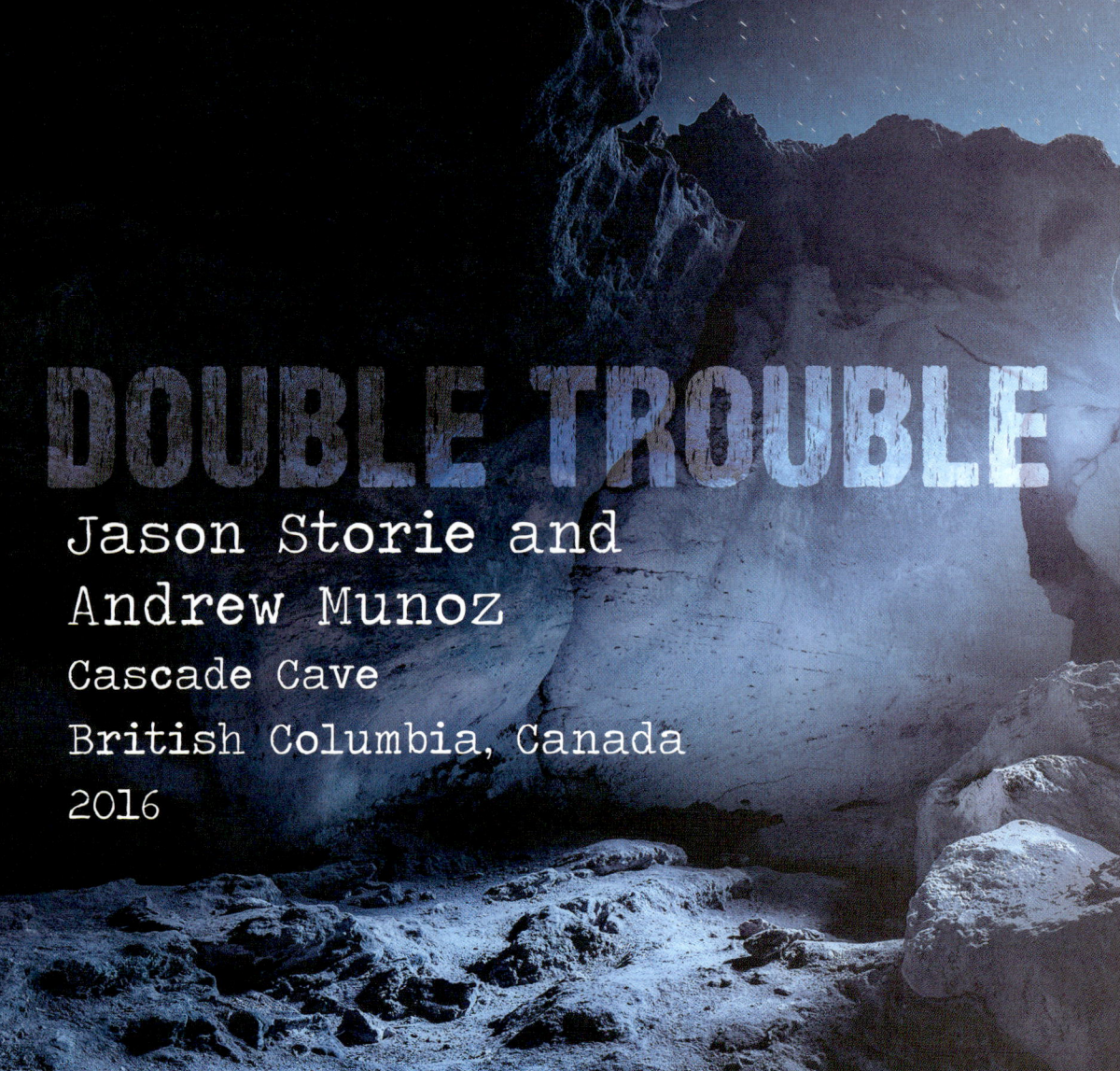

DOUBLE TROUBLE

Jason Storie and
Andrew Munoz
Cascade Cave
British Columbia, Canada
2016

Cascade Cave is located in Horne Lake Caves Provincial Park, in British Columbia, Canada.

Cascade Cave is located in British Columbia, Canada. And it is not a cave for beginners. The entrance to the cave has a large metal door. No one can enter without a special key. Cavers who want to explore must find out from other spelunkers how to get inside. "This is not a cave for first-timers," said Andrew Munoz. He explored the cave with Jason Storie in December 2016. "They said it was easy to get hurt in the caves. They also mentioned it was easy to destroy parts of the caves if explorers weren't very careful." He added, "Damage done in one second can be visible for ten thousand years."

Andrew and Jason traveled 200 feet (61 meters) below Earth's surface. But then, floodwaters from a storm aboveground flooded a challenging passageway. It is called Double Trouble. Cavers must pass through Double Trouble to leave the cave. When Double Trouble flooded, there was no way out.

"I found Jason on his back facing the top of the cave, almost up to his neck in the water."

ANDREW MUNOZ

SURVIVING THE CAVE 31

TRAPPED

The other cavers in the group made it through Double Trouble, but Jason was swept away by the flood. Andrew, a **paramedic** and an expert caver, rushed after his friend to help.

"I found Jason on his back facing the top of the cave, almost up to his neck in the water," said Andrew. "It was starting to come up around his ears and wash over him. It was draining his strength quickly because the water was so cold."

The men found shelter on a ledge. Andrew used a pocket stove to warm water. He poured it down Jason's caving suit to try to warm him up.

"Andrew and I were jammed into that crevice with a waterfall coming through that tunnel from floor to ceiling, like a giant fire hose," said Jason. "We had a space blanket just wide enough to cover the two of us," he added. For the next 14 hours, the men could only hope that their friends had made it to the surface and had gone for help. There was no way to know for sure.

paramedic: a person trained to give emergency medical care

Rain water can fill a cave in a matter of hours, and can cut off escape in minutes.

SURVIVING THE CAVE 33

HARD TO FIND

The cavers who had made it through Double Trouble called for help. More than 50 rescuers gathered at the cave's entrance. Divers went in to try to find Andrew and Jason. At one point, rescuers were only 25 feet (7.6 m) away from the stranded cavers. But the gushing water and complete darkness made it impossible for the trapped men to know that help was so close. The rescuers could not move forward in the flooded tunnel. They turned back.

After 14 hours, Andrew and Jason thought the water level was low enough for them to try to escape on their own. They made their way to the exit. They came out of the cave just as their rescuers were about to start a second rescue attempt. Andrew called up, "Hello!" One of the rescuers called back, "We love you!" They threw a rope down to Andrew and Jason and pulled them to safety.

RESCUE TEAMS

Two rescue groups in Canada—Alberta/British Columbia Cave Rescue Service and the Alberta Cave Rescue Organization—work together to help when cavers are trapped. They respond when people like Andrew and Jason need help inside North American caves. Cavers who enjoy spelunking as a hobby donate to the rescue program and take part in their training exercises. It's important to have experienced cavers and divers on a caving rescue team.

Of the millions of people who visit caves in the United States each year, about 50 become lost, stranded, or seriously injured.

LOCATION
Cascade Cave, Port Alberni, British Columbia, Canada

BRITISH COLUMBIA

SURVIVING THE CAVE 35

THE STUFF OF SURVIVAL

Surviving underground is not easy. Even simple supplies can help people survive while they wait for rescue. These are some of the resources that can help save lives.

GUIDELINE
A guideline is a rope that serves as a guide for cavers if they cannot see. Some caves that have regular visitors have permanent guidelines installed.

EXTRA OXYGEN
Cavers must always have a spare supply of air if they are going into a cave that is underwater. Many cave divers follow the rule of thirds: use one-third of the air to explore the cave, one-third of the air to return to safety, and save the extra third to use in case of an emergency.

LIGHT
Cavers must have several sources of light in case flashlight batteries go out or a light or lantern breaks or is lost.

BUDDY
Cavers must never enter a cave alone; they must always have at least one buddy, or teammate, with them.

RATIONS
Cavers never know when disaster can strike. Cavers must have extra food and water with them in case they are trapped inside.

SURVIVING THE CAVE 37

IRON WILL STATS

More than **2 million bats** live in the Monfort Bat Sanctuary in the Philippines. They live tightly packed into a 245-foot (75-m) cave.

Fewer than **100** people have explored the **5.5 million-year-old** Movile Cave in Romania because its air is poisonous. Strange species of spiders and scorpions that can live without oxygen or sunlight have been found in Romania's poison cave.

A dripping goo called "**snottite**" was discovered in a toxic cave in Tabasco, Mexico. Snottite is made of bacteria and acid. It's like a stalactite, but it's drippy instead of solid.

Son Doong Cave in Vietnam is one of the largest caving systems in the world. Some of the caverns are so large they could hold a **40-story skyscraper**.

The Hranice Abyss in the Czech Republic is the **deepest underwater cave** on Earth. An underwater robot measured a depth of **1,325 feet** (404 m). The cave was deeper, but the robot could go no further.

The Krubera Cave in Georgia in eastern Europe is the **deepest cave on Earth**. It descends **7,208 feet** (2,197 m) beneath Earth's surface and is **8.3 miles** (13.4 km) long.

An accident at a copper and gold mine trapped **33** miners **2,300 feet** (700 m) underground near Copiapó, Chile, on August 5, 2010. The miners survived for a record-breaking **69 days** before their rescue on October 13, 2010.

The **olm salamander** lives in caves in Croatia and Slovenia in Europe. The salamander has **no eyes**. It lives its entire life underground in the dark.

CAVE SYSTEMS

Being a cave explorer comes with many risks. Sudden flooding, tight passageways, and a pitch-black environment all add to the thrill—and the danger. No matter how many people enter and never return, these popular caves continue to welcome visitors.

1. MAMMOTH CAVE NATIONAL PARK

Kentucky, United States

Every year, more than 2 million people visit Mammoth Cave National Park in Kentucky. Visitors can explore 14 miles (23 km) of cave trails. About 600,000 visitors to the park go on ranger-led cave tours each year.

2. WAITOMO GLOWWORM CAVES

North Island, New Zealand

The Waitomo Glowworm Caves are covered in unique glowworms that can only be found in New Zealand. Most visitors take a 45-minute guided tour to see the beautiful glowworms that cover the walls and ceiling.

3. EGYPT'S BLUE HOLE

Dahab and Sinai, Egypt

Egypt's Blue Hole is one of the most dangerous underwater caves in the world. About 130 people have died exploring the Blue Hole over a 15-year period. Memorial plaques to lost divers cover the cliff face leading to the dive site.

4. THE TEMPLE OF DOOM

Tulum, Mexico

To enter this underwater cave, divers must jump into a deep hole in the ground. There is no path to the entrance. The cave is incredibly dark and filled with tight passages. Many divers have gotten lost and run out of air while exploring.

SURVIVING THE CAVE

IRON WILL

Cavers who travel deep beneath Earth's surface discover beautiful underground waterfalls and caverns made of crystal. Some cavers have discovered ancient statues and other works of art. Some have even found human mummies! Others have discovered strange species of animals and insects.

Rare natural wonders hide in dark, secret places deep underground. Cavers with a sense of adventure can see these unique and mysterious sites. But cavers know that they must work together to explore these dangerous places. Experienced cavers respect the danger that lurks underground. They prepare for emergencies and help one another in times of trouble. They know that only cavers with an iron will can survive when disaster strikes.

Caves are often beautiful and unique places to explore, but they can also be very dangerous if you are unprepared. Having the right equipment is equally as important as the iron will to survive.

SURVIVING THE CAVE 43

QUIZ

1 What was the name of the Thai soccer players' team?

2 How did the soccer team's coach help them to stay calm?

3 What is a Sked?

4 What trapped Andrew Wight's crew deep inside the cave?

5 How did Lukas Cavar become trapped in Sullivan Cave?

6 Which British diver helped rescue the Thai soccer team and the CSCA expedition in Cueva Alpazat, Mexico?

7 What type of job was Andrew Munoz trained to do?

8 What was the name of the flooded passageway that blocked Andrew Munoz and Jason Storie's escape?

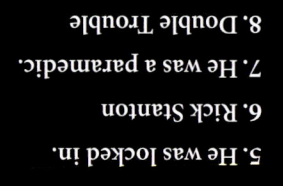

ANSWERS

1. The Wild Boars 2. He taught them how to meditate. 3. A waterproof, sleeping-bag-like container 4. Floodwaters and rubble 5. He was locked in. 6. Rick Stanton 7. He was a paramedic. 8. Double Trouble

ACTIVITY

Imagine you and your friends are exploring a deep underground cave. Suddenly, a rainstorm occurs aboveground. This causes flooding and a cave collapse. You only have two minutes to grab three life-saving items before rubble falls and traps your team underground.

MATERIALS NEEDED
- Paper
- Pen or pencil

STEPS
1. Choose items from these stories that will help you stay alive and call for help. Which items did you choose?
2. Write three short paragraphs explaining why you would choose each item.
3. Share with another group, or your friends or family.
4. Explain the importance of each item and why you have chosen it.

SURVIVING THE CAVE

GLOSSARY

condensation: water from the air that has settled onto a cool surface

fetal position: the way a baby curls up in its mother's womb; a position that helps conserve body heat

flash flood: a sudden, unexpected flood caused by heavy rain

foreign: from another country

gear: items such as tools, safety equipment, and other supplies needed to complete a task

immigration: the act of moving from one country to another

iron will: having a strong feeling that you are going to do something and that you will not allow anything to stop you

ledge: a narrow, flat surface that juts out from a rock wall

magma: hot liquid from below Earth's surface; lava and igneous rock are formed from magma

meditate: to spend time thinking quietly in order to reflect on something or to relax

monk: a religious person who separates from society to practice a spiritual way of living

paramedic: a person trained to give emergency medical care

ration: a supply of food

rubble: broken fragments of rock

sedated: given medicine to decrease pain or to soothe anxiety

spelunker: a person who explores caves

stalactite: a formation shaped like an icicle made from calcium salts that hangs from the ceiling of a cave

stalagmite: a mound or column made from calcium salts that rises from the floor of a cave

sump: a pit where water collects

tethered: tied to something

READ MORE

Best, B.J. *How Are Caves Formed?* Nature's Formations. New York: Cavendish Square Publishing, 2018.

Bodden, Valerie. *Caves.* Creep Out. Mankato, Minn.: Creative Education, 2018.

Honders, Christine. *Cave Geologists.* Out of the Lab: Extreme Jobs in Science. New York: PowerKids Press, 2016.

Labrecque, Ellen. *Caves.* Learning about Landforms. Chicago: Capstone Heinemann Library, 2014.

MacLeod, Elizabeth. *Secrets Underground: North America's Buried Past.* New York: Annick Press, 2014.

INTERNET SITES

https://www.nature.nps.gov/geology/usgsnps/cave/cave.html
Read about the fundamentals of geology, including the rocks and minerals found in caves.

https://www.businessinsider.com/thai-cave-rescue-timeline-how-it-unfolded-2018-7
Read an in-depth timeline of the 2018 Tham Luang cave rescue story.

https://easyscienceforkids.com/all-about-caves
Explore fun facts, vocabulary, a video, and more about caves.

https://www.lolwot.com/10-unexpected-things-found-in-caves-around-the-world
Learn about the fascinating and surprising things that people have built inside caves.

https://www.discoverydcode.com/dcode/articles/7-ways-survive-cave
Review different ways to survive if trapped inside a cave.

INDEX

Alpazat Caves 24–29

bats 20, 21, 38
Blue Hole 41

Cascade Cave 30–35
Cave of the Crystals 28
Combined Services Caving Association (CSCA) 25, 26, 28

divers 10, 11, 26, 34, 36, 41

flooding 7, 8, 9, 10, 13, 14, 25, 26, 29, 31, 32, 34, 40

Hranice Abyss 39

Krubera Cave 39

Mammoth Cave 23, 40

Nullarbor Plain 13, 16, 17

Pannikin Plains Caves 12–17

Son Doong Cave 38
spelunking 5, 22, 31, 34
stalactites 5, 8, 38
stalagmites 5
Sullivan Cave 18–23

Temple of Doom 41
Tham Luang caves 6–11, 26

Waitomo Glowworm Caves 40